This

poems by

Theodore Eisenberg

Finishing Line Press
Georgetown, Kentucky

This

Copyright © 2017 by Theodore Eisenberg
ISBN 978-1-63534-144-7 First Edition
All rights reserved under International and Pan-American Copyright Conventions. No part of this book may be reproduced in any manner whatsoever without written permission from the publisher, except in the case of brief quotations embodied in critical articles and reviews.

ACKNOWLEDGMENTS

Grateful acknowledgment is made to the publications in which the following poems first appeared, some in different form.

"Signs and Wonders" in *Rattle*
"Satchmo" in *The Aurorean*
"ID" in *Thema*
"Falsetto" in *Podium*

Publisher: Leah Maines

Editor: Christen Kincaid

Author Photo: David Prince

Cover Design: Elizabeth Maines McCleavy

Printed in the USA on acid-free paper.
Order online: www.finishinglinepress.com
also available on amazon.com

Author inquiries and mail orders:
Finishing Line Press
P. O. Box 1626
Georgetown, Kentucky 40324
U. S. A.

Table of Contents

Signs and Wonders 1
Om 2
Nightshade 3
Bus Stop 4
Where Trees Begin 5
Satchmo 6
Recessional 7
Flickers 8
David 9
Joseph Goes Down to San Joaquin 10
Rip Van Winkle 11
Hopscotch 12
Color Bind 13
PeepPeep—Her Feathers Felt 14
ID 15
Nightlight 16
Gulf of Eden 17
Come to Maine He Said 19
Sistine Chapel 20
Minotaur 21
Burial Site 22
Bloodhound 23
Sunspot 24
Falsetto 25
Sis 26
Hitchcock 27
The Lamp 28
Vesper 29
Wolverine 30

*In memory of Jack Eisenberg —
recalling my first poetry, the cadence of his voice.*

Signs and Wonders

If the dance of a leaf in the wind
is not a woman in disguise,
then I am not a man,
and know nothing of holiness.

If the wind is not a plea
to change my ways,
the sap of maple
not an expression of mother's milk,
the autumn rain
not a lament for Adam;
if papers dropped by strangers
are only papers,
and not reminders,
and peeling paint not portent;
if dreams are only dreams,
and not stories my father neglected;
if leaves in the wind won't gather?

Om

Adz chops a confessional…

Burly masses, connives meshed
fabric. Dilettante—moth nibbles.
Eerie moon-breaths flip sun-ups.
Glib otters from the daily O.

Hillbillies pluck goat strings, imp toes
with angel dust. *Jour* days your life, keen
as a serrated edge. Lung blows a fish into
your chest, miff mistaking a whiff for grace.

Norm smacks you right—oink, oink
muddy sex. Pulley childs a tug. Quip
the foreskin of your c'mon. Rake
prongs haunts, sweats copper into fitting.

Tinsel adores an alpine queen of hearts;
uppity snubs soles of feet—vogue
comeuppance of her sizzling eye—
wily, slyly slinking winking hips.

Xenon flashes traces
of rare self; yen
compresses you into
want. Zen finds you…

Nightshade

Drones, invisible as angel
wings of dragonflies,
approach in a crook
of black forest shadow,
soak the flesh of heaven
in belladonna, cling in fire;
kinderlach spark and glow.

Bus Stop

Seventy is a cold skin.

A plague of age inhabits city streets,
cracking sidewalks; insinuates itself
into the city reservoir, rusting pipes.

I take a bus to children's play.

To hide and seek. Their tag is upon me,
and I am it, or will be soon. At night,
a ghost moon musters a new report.

February.

Where Trees Begin

A paw reminds me
that I am sought,
not in a distracted way,
as I might speak
to a distant relative,
but deep in the pink
of his mouth.
A joyous tongue licks
salt from my skin.
Rough leather pads walk
over outstretched legs,
rasping my knees.
A wet nose pokes,
refusing my solitude.
Now! He throws his
wait against the door,
his front paws against
all that is contained.

Satchmo

This song is squirrel
stopping—starting,
evasive.
Acorns fall on rock
and roll—dance
the rhythm of the oak.
A shingle of bark stirs,
then leaps—
this autumn jazz.

Recessional

thimble of ash,
feather weight,

how it held
with wire feet,

how it jagged,

orange stripes
on its wings,

on its wings
a flute.

Flickers

North of Swansea, south
of Llanelli, in the inward
face of the Carmarthen Bay,
salt marsh of the Burry Inlet
homes godwit, whimbrel
and the common scoter.

In Angelsey, beyond
Fishguard, roseate terns
the day. Black kites. Merlins
cast the night. Dowitchers.
Swifts hasten shrikes. On
and on the feathered sky.

David

The sky is failing.
I ask the red hen
if this is so.
Bedlam, she says,
they have eaten
my loaves, dispirited
my help, raided
the porridge.
My cupboard barren
as old shoes, my
entrance way crooked
miles. Lambs
have claimed the
hills and are bleating.
Take this shepherd's pipe;
gather them home.

Joseph Goes Down to San Joaquin

I believe in dreams, although my
parents never farmed in California.
I soak up my father in the rambling
house. Its reddened boards, seared
above the altar, where sacrifices
are received. Uncles wander
through, bed in unfinished pine.
These rooms sealed with masking
tape. Outside, chickens; a grey inspector
slaps a fine for farming without
permit, beyond what can be paid.
No one feeds the fowl, which
multiply like hares (my mother
sheer). Creatures cohabit in puce
sheds; rising mist of chicken down.
The inspector grabs one by the wattles
and the comb, ripping it in two;
points to a sign, *unwelcome*; slurs
my paternal name. From cypress
limb an owl swoops by. A cry
cascades outward from the coops.

Rip Van Winkle

was not asleep when what
he knew left for other times;
what loved him back;
when what he saw was flat
and faceless as a door;
his was a sleepy town; days
short and nights dragged on
in dreaming; he, himself,
a dreamer, remembering this
and that, whether they had
or had not been, but memories
all the same, and real as what
he touched with an open hand,
in his deepest dream, her neck
perhaps, or ear; he knew he
neither slept nor left, but
stood in the stream alone,
fish fleeing from his steps,
a breeze spiriting away his scent.

Hopscotch

She scratches streets,
maps her future in boxes,
pebbles squares,
bundling time in tens.
Her dance brings bees;
that she is one.
Her footfall jounces
earthy haunts. From
cracks of asphalt
feelers emerge, search
chalk for safety.
From a sewer grate
a raccoon peers,
daylight his suspicion.
She calls; that door
is shut. After night
has bedeviled sky,
she shares darkness
with bandit eyes.

Color Bind

When I attended your exhibition,
my dog sniffed out the orange
blossoms on your neck. I bought
your painting, *Fifty Tintorettos
of Blue*, each shade opening to
another shade, and to its window,
until the sky—translucent with
the stain of late afternoon—ended.

Now you withdraw into blue
night sheets and the blue night
wood of your table; you haunt
pictures with blue oils from your
hands. Your blue spores dormant
in the pocket of my sea shirt
of blue chanteys, where I keep
a log on slips of blue sea.

PeepPeep—Her Feathers Felt

I receive her breath and breathe it back inside her,
while canine teeth tusk in pink dark,
sing of a lilac bush within a swathe of mink.

Sofia kicks her foreign sandals off;
when she bends over, I think she thinks of me.
Mozart keys her stand in freshets of ivory.

Her down fondles a newborn chick;
in ever-glades I part reeds and utter.
Blood runs from slaughter,

Reddens my feet. Among wet greens
of overnights I think too much of dying,
taste brine within her mouth.

Her salamander flicks, shirking a single pose.
A magpie, Scheherazade, sings to save
each day—Musknightvanillaflowers.

Bo Derek speaks; a great white eats her.
She finds the hammer in my ear
the way Georgia peaches open.

ID

A man with a suitcase
sits on a wooden bench.
If I call him Charley, you
may think him a chump,
dozing at the station,
after missing his train,
a shiny diesel. Perhaps
he waits on his love, who
freshens in the powder room.
Or he may be your uncle
from Syracuse, who never
succeeded; what he never tried
contributes to his failure.
Or your brother, who tried
his luck in Vegas. Don't
leave him with no place
to go at night. The cops
will force him to the street,
the last home for a lost man.
Did I say a man? Perhaps
a child, the son you disregarded.
You think of him often, traveling
to the station with your bag,
as if knowing where to look.

Nightlight

I do not replace my pug
with a second Sparky,
but as family, give
his vacancy a name
at the table.

You think I write about
a dog—you who lost
everyone at Treblinka,
who cannot remember
yourself, let alone your
mother's torn-away arms,
your wall of lesions.

Gulf of Eden

Day 1.
After she died,
the carpet lay bruised
beside a yellow chair,
pushed to a white wall
by what he should
have done. For staring.
Outside, rhododendrons
shrank the sun to splinters.

Day 2.
He thinks green
green, that he knows
grey; blue comes
by sea, surreptitiously;
you know nothing,
it spits, *even grey
incipient.*

Day 3.
Rain mocks
the helpless roof,
drips into giants;
his own sky sets them
down above his bare
head; a vine grows
through him.

Day 4.
Thou shall not eat the eagle,
the bearded vulture with
its savior, the osprey lifting
water from the firmament,
the glebe, kites and their kin
he watches against the light,
the horned owl that hoots

the strangle-dark that hunts
the lame, lengths of heron
straw a sickened marsh,
the hoopoe is unknown,
bats sense hope and flock him.

Day 5.
He must wear hemp
and hanging thread,
remember ever and the day
that follows; never relent—
never uncover, ungirdle
his thigh, his chest,
his unholy head, his nape.

Day 6.
Ceiling sparks,
a metal finger reaches
up; he drives to bang,
to crash his rage; there's
no more to the ride
than that, what he inflicts
and what assails him.

Day 7.
Canisters of hard plastic
—horse radish, hardened
yolks, old bones, apples
smashed to sauce, latch
keys, figurines placed
in towers. She in one—
he speaks for the first time
—she would have known
he meant it—and he trapped
within another. He would
walk   a thread to her.

Come to Maine He Said

The end of spring, red ash.
His wife, his Irish auburn lass—
some miles north of town.
He lay red tulips down, waited
for his pips, his garnet eyes,
to dry, before we turned to
see the bay throw back its wake.

Waves massed at land's retreating
line, twelve feet above their ebb.
The startled shore, stoned beach
—chromasia. Pigments broken
off a bluff, sanded by sea salt.
One stone sidled with the tide
and showed its face to me.

A child's face—its stunted chin
and elevated brow—to me.
Its pin-prick eyes and ever-smoothing
cheeks—to me.
Its supplication in my hand,
beneath the imprint of my digits,
my singularity.

To you, heir to this remain,
I pass this icon, Margaret, Icarus
—this boy, my guess/my swoon.
 I hand this *wonderstone*—
    its sea   sky earth
    its   plea and now
to you to answer to.

Sistine Chapel

When I attended
death attached
fatherscent
like pollen.
Sometimes
his wide eyes
moved, his hand
clutched a wrinkle
of sheet to raise it,
his gown opened.
On the ceiling
I taped a poster
of The Creation.
Adam touched
god's hand
each day
for months.

Minotaur

A writer visits the family
lock-up, his mother spliced,
as cut cable. A bison-
headed monster roams
the ward at night; what
she imagines to be real.

A cold wall begins to melt.
To the east, a toy trawler
trolls for a golden fish. He
leaps cracks to a buzzer
and its metallic door,
pursued by her amazement.

Burial Site

Geese rise to the sky
at once, announcing
not only themselves,
but that death does
not surround me.
I am an isthmus
between raised wings
and stones which
configure into families.
My feet sink into
earth, soft as a belly.
While driving north,
I see my body.

Bloodhound

Premonition as hound,
tracking your day, sniffing
the consciousness of night.
There comes a time when it is true,
when it was what it will be.
Your book of borrowed pages.
Next. Father, mother and finally,
terminally, you. Now nothing is true.
(Nothing is true). Your grey report
in your own hand; your mind
grinds shark cartilage, stops
to scratch before crossing.

Sunspot

The caravan's intention, haste;
its circumstance, sand. It moves
in humped swaying, resembling
hiccoughs. Its contest, sun.
Winds ensure it wasn't there.
Upon arrival, water and lying
about. No design—no caravan.

Falsetto

Stone-by-stone, a house constructs
a view above the water line. Stone
strictures constrain each side, impelling
falls. I watch remains from the impending
thirties. Whether 3 or 5, one carved number
will not spell. My companion says *WPA*.
My father, then a boy, had he been alive
today. The dead have never lived; argon.
Continuing ... before *The War* they
did not know. Old beauties these stones.
I am about to ask, *WPA?* He stares,
supposing me. Light-stricken streams
plunge and tumble only to resume.
Bubbles breathe below. If there are fish,
I do not see them. I fear my glasses
will leap, follow what I cannot see.

Sis

O I could be dad, reading
in the tub. I could be reading
Whitman to the water fall.
Through wisps of steam
above the water line, I could
watch grey chest hair curl.
Louder, I could say to his song.

In the cataract, reciting
Paumanok, Mannahatta ...
I'm no *o voluptuous cool-
breathed* lover in the tub,
but could pen the margin,
turning leaves of grass to
grant my song's self pardon.

Hitchcock

You talk about death,
and you talk about
death, until terror
struts into your home,
plump as a cameo,
sits at your table,
steeps tea.

Your nurse,
a maniac,
slices your pillow,
pours bleach on your feet.
Your parents' photograph
of your boyish self
falls in a fizzle of down.

The Lamp

From afar a baby crows. Egret within
the pause before evening. A path around
Veronica Lake—algae feeding on ripples
and flow. An aide from the islands leads
four wheels, below crossed bars with sure-
grip handles—before a man, whose right
foot never overtakes his left.

Recall your retriever, his back legs buckled
when he rose to his name, never had he
not answered at attention. He dragged
his back-half to the corner, behind the couch.

I implore my aide to sing of night breezes
from her island, that drew her brother
into currency. Not of piranha, that claimed
two toes before he returned to shore.
Of *tremolo* that drew him from beneath
trapped swelter, athirst, before sleep,
past snakes that slithered with abandon.

Once, my genie read something like that
to me, before bed, before we children were
—each one—kidnapped and held—transomed
away from light, some to eighty, and beyond.

Vesper

Each spring, some
years—each day, I
bird-dog each tree,
how each differs
from yesterday, to
snag each bloom.

I best love white birch;
to touch its paper-
bark confession.

To say—*sky streaked
in glory*, even if
I speak in amaranths,
cannot describe
(what's dew) what
I see in fleeing light.

Wolverine

Gulo, Gulo.
You mustelid, luscus gulon.
Your sauntering blades
low against the earth.

Carcajou, carcajou.
Come glutton;
break this frame of bone.
Feast on the organ playing.

Theodore Eisenberg's life as a poet began at age four, learning to recite Kipling's *The Ballad of East and West,* as his father read from the bathtub. After college at Cornell, he veered toward the pragmatic, attending Georgetown Law. His legal career blossomed into more than anticipated, as he became managing partner of Grotta, Glassman and Hoffman, a labor law firm in New Jersey, which ultimately merged with a national firm, Fox Rothschild LLP.

Along the way, he undertook leadership positions in the environmental movement and within the Jewish community. More importantly, he married Karen, his wife of forty years, and had four children, followed by five grandchildren and counting. In 2014, he retired from the practice of law, after 38 years, to return to poetry—the unrealized aspiration of his childhood. His poems have appeared, or will appear, in *The Listening Eye, Midstream, Jewish Currents, The Aurorean, Podium, Poetica, Thema, Rattle, Halfway Down the Stairs, Slipstream Press, Crosswinds Press* and *The Ragged Sky Anthology.* This is the first book arising from that first inkling.

www.ingramcontent.com/pod-product-compliance
Lightning Source LLC
LaVergne TN
LVHW041509070426
835507LV00012B/1450